MISSING
Puzzle PIECES

Ann J. Mann

MISSING
Puzzle PIECES

Published by
DQ Spirit Works, LLC
Dayton, OH

Copyright © 2017 by Ann J. Mann

All rights reserved.

No part of this book may be reproduced, stored in a retrieval system, or transmitted in any form or by any means – electronic, mechanical, photocopying, recording, or otherwise – without prior permission in writing from the copyright holder except provided by USA copyright law.

Scripture quotations marked NKJV are from the Holy Bible, New King James Version. Copyright © 1982 by Thomas Nelson, Inc. Used by permission. All rights reserved.

Scripture quotations marked NIV are from
THE HOLY BIBLE, NEW INTERNATIONAL VERSION ®, NIV ® Copyright © 1973, 1978, 1984, 2011 by Biblica, Inc.TM Used by permission. All rights reserved worldwide.

ISBN-13: 978-0-986-35881-4

First American Paperback Edition

Printed in the United States of American

Foreword

Originally, I intended to write my story so I could give it to my children, as a part of their legacy. My history is their history, and there are parts of this that they have never heard.

With the encouragement of my husband, Jim, supporting me as I tell my story, and the enthusiasm of a friend from church, this story has grown bigger than I ever imagined.

I hope my story might help and encourage someone who is attempting their own journey.

A special thank you to Stephanie and Stewart Halfacre. With their encouragement I was able to compile the pieces of the puzzles and turn it into a legacy.

Are You My Mother?

I've been looking for you for 31 years. Maybe now you will read my story and find me*
By Claudia Jean Truax

It isn't just on Mother's Day that I think of you and wonder if you are happy, healthy, and enjoying your life. Every day, for as long as I can remember, you have been in my thoughts and my dreams and I have longed so to know you.

Have you been able to forget me? I sincerely doubt that you could forget your own flesh and blood. It was 31 years ago last December, in a scruffy little coal-mining town in Pennsylvania, that we parted—on your wishes, not mine. I've been told that you named me after one of the nuns of St. Joseph who had showed you kindness during your confinement. Can you understand how that saddens me? To think that you were so hungry for a little kindness that you so honored a stranger.

Perhaps I have misinterpreted, but I'm sure you can forgive me if I have, because you must remember that I know nothing of your circumstances, your background, or YOU.

Of course, the people who adopted me changed my name. I also now have my married name, but somehow I still identify very strongly with the name you gave me.

I trust that you did what you felt was best, and I have no anger inside me. What I do have is a terrible void that compels me to search the face of every older woman I meet to look for something—a dimple, a mannerism—that would indicate that she could be the woman who gave me life.

I wonder which of my talents are gifts from you. Do you love music as I do? Have I you to thank for my love of poetry, animals, literature? And my two beautiful children—which of them most closely resembles their unknown grandmother?

I've spent so many years trying to find you. Either my sleuthing abilities are lacking, or you have no wish to be found. I find the latter difficult to understand because I have no wish to intrude upon your privacy or interfere with any new life you have built for yourself. I only want to know you, to comfort you if you need comforting, to see the woman whose blood courses through my veins and those of my children, to help you if I can—to put my arms around my mother, if only for an instant.

On this Mother's Day and every other day of every other year, I hope you realize that whoever you are and wherever you might be, I love you. Thank you for all that you have given me, and anything you might have given up for me.

Your loving daughter,
Claudia

Tell The Child He Was CHOSEN For Adoption

BY MARCIA WINN.

THIS INQUIRY came in the mail: How can we tell our adopted child that he is adopted?

For 10 years, this mother wrote, she and her husband had hoped to have a baby. Finally they adopted one and came to love him "as dearly as though he had been ours." Soon, as is not uncommon, they realized they were going to have another baby, this time of their own flesh and blood.

But how to tell the first child, now four years old and very precious to them, that he was adopted? Until the new baby appeared iminent, they had not felt the need of it. Would he be hurt? Could he be made to understand that really, truly, they loved him very much, that he was their own son?

Often the simplest acts are the most difficult, especially with children. Tell him the truth. Don't wait for someone else to tell him. Tell him your house was the emptiest place in the world until he came; that after he came, your house became so warm and loving that you wanted another baby for him to play with, that you sought him out because you so terribly wanted him.

★ ★ ★

THOSE EXPERIENCED in placing children for adoption say that the wisest course is to start the story of adoption as soon as possible. Never attempt to disguise or hide it. Let the child know that the word "adopted" means "We picked you out," and that being adopted is being loved.

The child usually will ask, "What is 'adopted'?"

The true answer, of course, is, "We wanted you."

The child usually should be told this between the ages of 3 and 4, always ___ he starts school. Say it ___ own way, but always m___ ___ear that

You and Your Child

you didn't adopt him for today or tomorrow, but for always, that he is your own, legally.

We heard of one family that found itself in a slight mess, however, by pointing out the glories of adoption. Their first and adopted child became so proud of his status—"They picked me out from a whole house full of babies and took me to court" — that when their second child, their own, was born and grew to be 4 or 5, adoption became such a pinnacle of aspiration that they had to take him to court and legally adopt him, too. Only then was he convinced that he belonged. This incredible story is true.

★ ★ ★

EXPERTS in the adoption field say that once you have told a child he is adopted, you should not wait for him to ask more. Spur his curiosity. Explain and repeat as often as necessary.

Tell him all about the nursery and how you went again and again hoping for him, the preparations you made for the happy day when you could take him home and how happy both he and you were once he was there. Do all this, but don't make adoption seem too superior to birth.

Whatever you say, they advise, be logical and be truthful. If disturbing factors are present, bring them out early and gradually. Describe his own parents vividly, if possible. Let him be as proud of them as he is of you.

Two-thirds of all adoptive parents, a survey showed, wonder how much to tell a child when he wants to know more about his real parents. Ordinarily the adoptive parent doesn't know too much to tell.

If, on the other hand, you can spot some similarity in him to you or his foster father or his foster relatives—his walk, his smile, his mannerisms, his blondness or his darkness—mention these often. He will like it. A child—as well as an adult—has to belong. He has to know, as we all have to know, that whatever he does, he is yours.

★ ★ ★

VARIOUS adopting parents use special techniques. One mother may use the word "adopted" in an improvised lullaby until it becomes a familiar and affectionate word. Another family may tell the story, set to nursery music, on a home recording machine; here again it becomes loved and familiar.

Others keep baby books starting out with "My Adoption Day," diaries chronicling the baby's arrival and progress, or scrapbooks that the child may pore over in later years. Through these the child will know that he always was part of a loving family.

(The next Child Care article will appear next Sunday).

—Constance Bannister Photo.

"Let the child know . . . that being adopted is being loved."

Missing Puzzle Pieces

MISSING PUZZLE PIECES

Jeremiah 1:5 —

Before I formed thee in the belly I knew thee

I don't know how far back the story began. The stage was set, players in place, long before I was born.

I do remember that I always knew I was adopted. My first memory was of my mom telling me I was "chosen." She told me the story of how she and my dad went to pick out a baby, because they wanted one so much. They walked down rows of babies. When they stopped at me, I reached out for my dad's finger. I had found my new family.

The First Pieces of My History

My adoptive grandmother was the oldest of six children and the only girl, born to Italian immigrants. As a young girl she was sent to Villa Marie Academy in Erie, PA. The family lived in Kane, PA, about 90 miles southeast of Erie. I believe there's a connection between my grandmother, Erie, people she might

■ Me and my parents

■ My dad holding me in front of our row house in Philadelphia. My grandmother is standing in the front door.

have known there and my adoption, but this will always be unknown.

Because they were Catholic, the priests were always an integral part of her family's life. Eventually, my grandmother married. She and her husband owned and operated a bakery in Kane, the first in that area to have a delivery truck. In her 30s my grandmother found herself a widow with two young daughters. For several years afterward, she ran the family bakery. My grandmother was a take-charge type of woman.

After graduating from high school, my mom studied at Hahnemann Medical School in Philadelphia, becoming a registered nurse. While in Philadelphia she met the love of her life, my dad. After they were married, my dad went off to World War II on the European front. My mom went back to Kane to work at the local hospital and to wait. After the war, my parents set up housekeeping in Philadelphia, hoping to start their family.

After several miscarriages, my parents began to consider adoption. My grandmother, who had worked for the church in Kane, spread the word that her daughter and husband wanted to adopt.

Father Downing, a longtime family friend and pastor at St. Ann's Church in Erie, shared with my grandmother that he knew of an infant available for adoption. My grandmother called my parents, telling them to take the first train they could get to Erie.

When I was two and a half weeks old, my parents were able to take me home.

On the return trip back to Philadelphia the train went through Kane, mom's hometown. While the train stopped at the station, the proud parents held their new baby daughter up to the window. Friends and family members had gathered on the platform to wave and to get a glimpse of the new family.

Missing Puzzle Pieces

LETTER TO AN
UNKNOWN MOTHER

I don't think of you very often. In fact, most of the time I make an effort to keep you out of my thoughts. And yet—sometimes—just before I drift off to sleep or when I look into my son's eyes I think of you.

I don't know you. Are you a woman? A girl of 16? Involved in a career? Married? In school? I don't know. There are so many reasons why you might have chosen to give your baby (now so very much our baby) away. Whatever your reasons it must have been a difficult decision and an even more difficult experience to live through. Even if you were able to make such a decision early in your pregnancy it must have been very hard to go through with it once the baby was born. I often feel sad for you...because it is sad to create something beautiful and then to be forced to turn your back on it.

You must have felt some love too...if not for the baby, perhaps for his father. You may have been a young girl experimenting with life or perhaps you were terribly lonely. In any case you weren't ready to become a parent...I was.

It is true, you are my son's mother. No, you are the woman who bore him (and I am sometimes jealous of you for this) but I am now his mother. I love him, "mother" him, live with him, care for him....

Surely you must wonder about me. I'd like you to know how very much we love our son and how grateful we are to you for being the life force that brought him into being. Thank you for giving him his big hazel eyes, his soft skin, his happy spirit, his bright mind. Thank you for giving us this child who is everything we had ever hoped for.

As time goes by you and I will think of each other less and less. You are starting your life anew—and hopefully will have another chance to gain happiness. We are finding fulfillment for our lives in our son. But...now...while you are still very much on my mind ...I want to say "thank you."

Later, three daughters – Margaret, Mary, and Elizabeth – were born to my parents. By then we had moved to New Jersey. Life was simple – riding bikes, roller-skating down the sidewalks, playing with paper dolls on the front porch. I had a wonderful childhood. But because I knew I was adopted, I always knew that there was another family out there, that missing piece of my life.

Even though I had questions, I never asked. When I would approach the subject of my adoption, it was always tactfully dismissed. My mom didn't understand my need to know who I really was – my feeling of aloneness in the midst of a demonstrative, happy family. My parents' answer was, "Why do you want to know? You have a family that loves you" or "You don't know what you'll find."

When I was about 12 or 13 years old, my Girl Scout troop took a trip to Savannah, GA. The day before we left I was up in the attic snooping and searching as usual. I came across an envelope with my adoption decree. The document reported that my name had been changed to Ann Jeanne Zell. But what had it been changed from? No identifying names or information regarding the birth family was included.

The document also contained this sentence: "Natural mother surrendered the child – her subsequent conduct amounted to an abandonment."

There I was, getting ready to depart on a trip that would take me hundreds of miles from my family, with the realization that I had been abandoned – not wanted. At that age, when I wanted to fit in, I felt alone, on the outside looking in. To this day, I hate the word abandoned.

In terms of appearance, I didn't look like the others in my family. My father was German and my mother Italian. Everyone in the family had dark brown eyes, and my mother and sisters were short. I was tall, with light hair and blue-green

Missing Puzzle Pieces

■ 1st birthday party. We lived in Philly.

■ Approximately 1963-64. Front of our home in Maple Shade, NJ.

Register of Wills Office, Form No. 45

State of Pennsylvania
County of Erie } ss.

I, Ralph B. McCord, Clerk of the Orphans' Court in and for the County of Erie, State of Pennsylvania, do hereby certify that the following is a true and correct copy of the Decree of Court in the Matter of the adoption of Clara Marie Betts as appears by the record in said case No. 7 In Adoption September Term, 1949.

Decree

And now, to-wit: September 30, 1949 the foregoing petition having been presented in court not less than ten days from this date, and it appearing that notice of the petition has been given to all persons who are required to be notified by law, and that the petitioners are desirous of adopting Clara Marie Betts as an heir and have shown their willingness to perform all the duties of parents to said child and that the consents required by law are in writing and annexed to the petition, and on consideration of the petition and testimony

and it appearing that the natural mother surrendered the child and gave a general consent to her adoption which, with her subsequent conduct amounted to an abandonment (see 104 Pa. Sup. 196 McCann);

And the Court, being satisfied that the statements made in the petition are true and that the welfare of said child will be promoted by her adoption, and that all the requirements of the Act, No. 93, of April 4, 1925, and amendments thereto, have been complied with, therefore decrees that the said Clara Marie Betts shall be the adopted child of G. William Zell and Ida Jane Zell and shall have all the rights of a child and heir of said petitioners and be subject to the duties of such child, and that said child shall henceforth assume the name of ANN JEANNE ZELL.

J. ORIN WAITE
President Judge

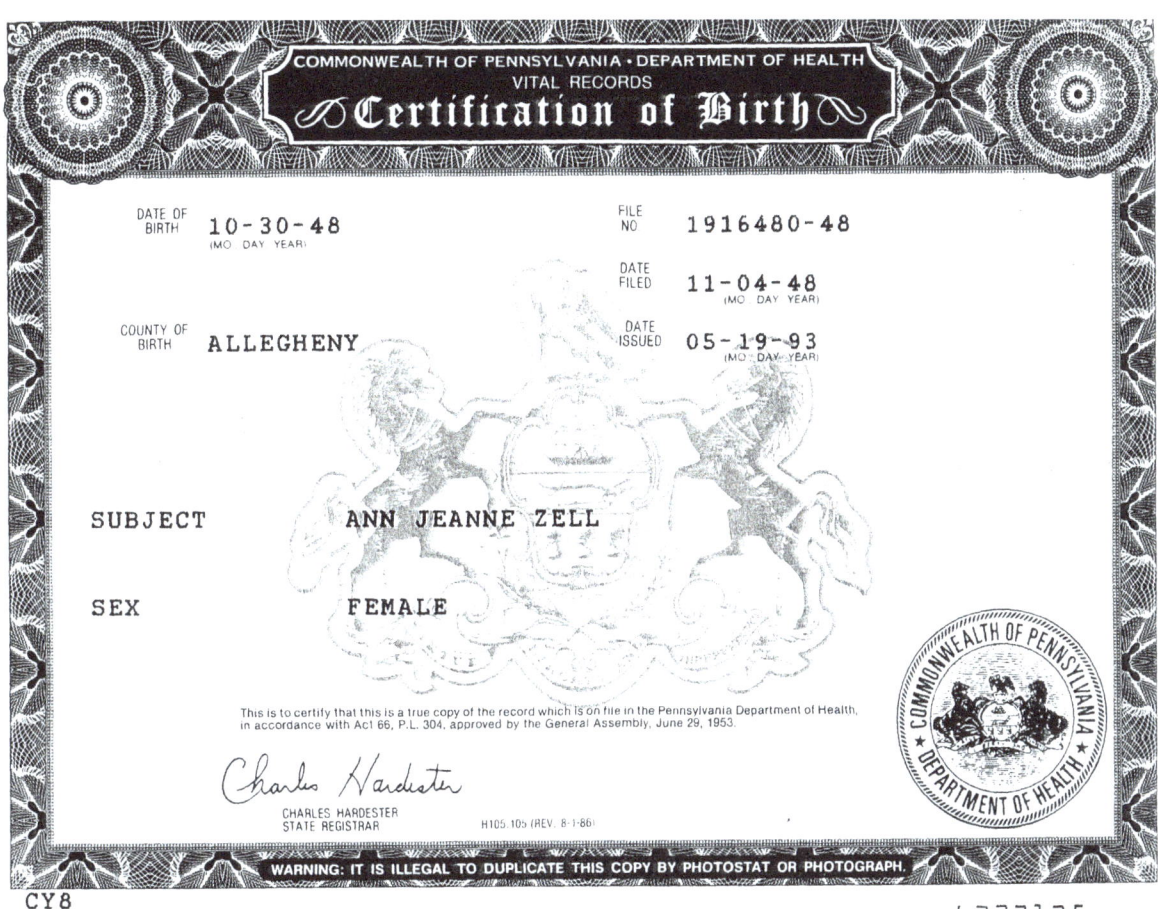

- My amended certificate of birth. Amended after the adoption.

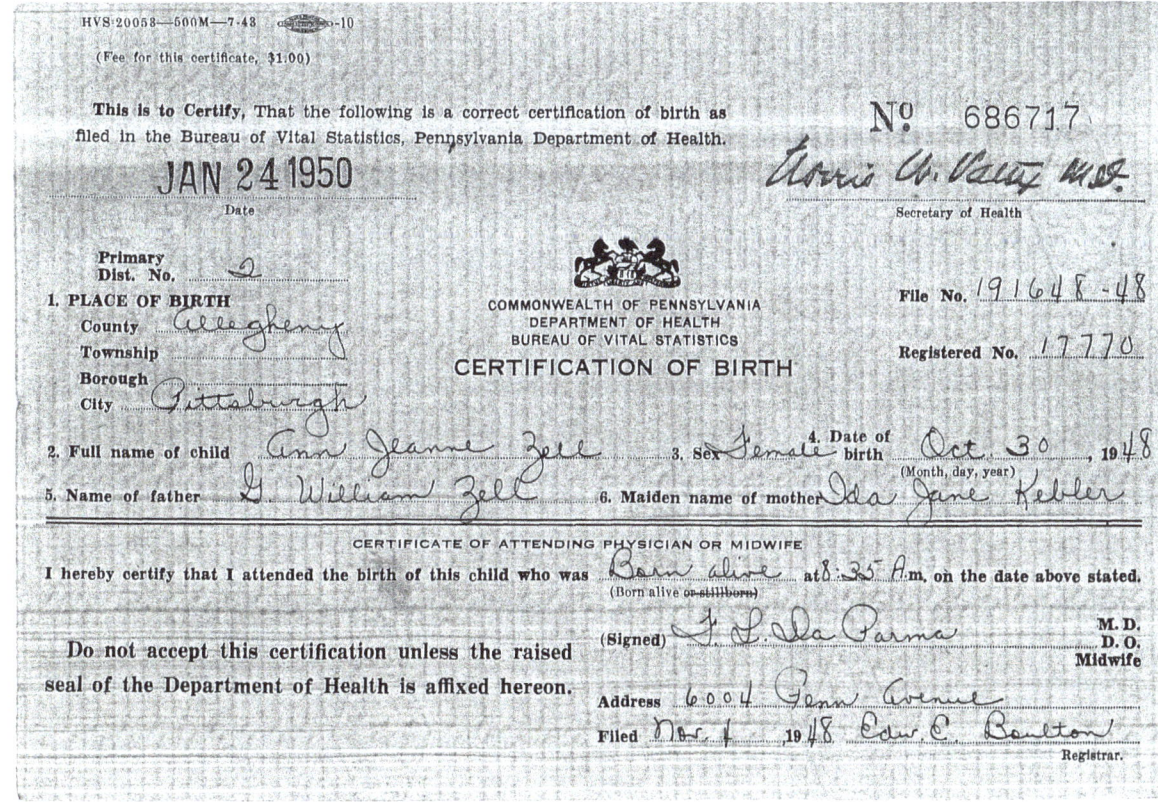

eyes. They were all demonstrative, while I was always an overly polite and reserved child, always the quiet one.

From childhood, through adolescence, and into my teens, I was always the people-pleaser, the good child. I didn't want to give anyone a reason to give me away again. That thought was so deeply ingrained into me that it was only during the past few years that I fully realized its impact. Even though I had the most loving family and a happy childhood, there were always missing puzzle pieces, which haunted me.

It is amazing now as I look back on what I call my self-realization period – why I acted and felt the way I did, the inferior feelings of not living up to someone else's expectations, the feeling of not belonging, feeling that I was on the outside looking in.

My senior year of high school, two months before graduation, my dad passed away. He went to the hospital and never came home. The evening he passed the hospital called. Mom answered the phone downstairs, and I answered it upstairs at the same time, surrounded by my three sisters. The voice on the other end of the phone reported, "Mrs. Zell, your husband has just expired" – as simple and matter-of-fact as that. Now what was going to happen to us. The next few days were a whirlwind.

After it was all over my uncle, who was a doctor, suggested I should be kept home from school for a few more days. He was concerned I hadn't shown much emotion. All along mom had been telling me that I was her pillar of strength and that she needed to be able to lean on me.

I have learned over the years the power that words have on us. Adopted, abandoned, pillar of strength – all words that helped build my walls of self protection and indifference. I started to believe that since I came into the world alone, that would be my destiny, to be alone.

Two years later, almost to the day my dad passed, mom's sister from College Corner Ohio was tragically killed – a traumatic happening. When we received the news, our grandmother, who was now living with us, went into temporary shock.

Once again, when dealing with a loss, I promised myself I'd be even stronger. I could handle it myself; nothing would ever affect me that way.

A couple of months after my aunt's funeral I decided I was going to venture out on my own. So off to Ohio I went. I can look back now and see how unsettled I was, always looking for those missing puzzles pieces.

My parents had never told my sisters I was adopted. She didn't want Margaret, Mary and Liz to think I was treated differently. I never told them either.

When I knew I was moving out I decided to tell my sisters. I told each sister individually. I don't remember what words I used, but I do remember the responses: Margaret: "I always knew you were different"; Mary: "Really, tell me how it feels"; Liz: "Annie, I still love you."

I moved to Oxford Ohio, home of Miami University. After finding a place to live and a job, I settled in to being on my own. There were many visits back to New Jersey, and phone calls several times a week. Ohio was a bit of a culture shock at first – everyone had an accent and they couldn't understand me.

After a couple of years, I married and then had two wonderful children, Bill and Kris. My pregnancies caused me to think about a different missing puzzle piece. What if there were genetic problems or health issues? I had all the "what if's" a new mother has, and more. This re-kindled the desire to search for my heritage.

There's a man and woman who gave me life. It's where I got my hazel eyes, brown curly hair and 5'8" stature. There's brothers and sisters I don't even know. Even though I had a wonderful childhood I always was aware there was another family, who's heredity I shared. I've always known the details and understood

I searched for 15 years and looked into many a stranger's eyes, wondering. ~~There's even the unanswered health questions~~

Though my name was changed, I was born Clara Maire Betts, Oct 30, 1948. My mother, Shirley Mae, born in Erie, is around 64. My father, James, born in New Rochelle, N.Y. would be about 76.

I don't want to intrude on anyone's life. If they would like to know me, I'd love to know them.

I'd like to thank both of you for my life, something that seems to hold little value now~~adays~~.
I love you
Clara Marie

■ One of the many attempts to make contact with my birth parents. A rough copy of a letter I was going to submit to an Erie newspaper, but never did.

In the late 70's I sent to the Pennsylvania Bureau Statistics for my unamended birth certificate. Finally, the envelope came. Finally, I had names. Birth father, James R. McGoey, was several years older than my birth mother, Shirley M. Betts. My birth name was Clara Maire Betts. Pennsylvania closed all adoption records not long after I received mine.

Since the parents' last names were different I figured I was the child of an unmarried relationship. Back in those days you didn't tell a child she was the result of an affair. I understood my mom's fairy tale version.

For a couple of days afterward I just wanted to keep looking at that piece of paper. I sent for an Erie, PA, phone book. There it was – name, address, and phone number of my birth father. For some reason, my birth father was important to me, perhaps because I had lost my dad but still had my mom at that time. Since I grew up in the era before computers, searching was limited. I did not ask questions of my parents or grandmother, perhaps out of respect, not wanting to hurt them, or perhaps because of the fear of the unknown.

Since I was raised Catholic, and a priest was one of the first pieces of this puzzle, I figured it was most likely a Catholic adoption. Now where would I go from there? I had an idea, a phone number, and a script of what I would say.

I called my birth father's house, during the day and spoke to his wife. I told her I was with the Catholic Telegraph, literature that was in every Catholic home. I was verifying their subscription and asked, "For our records, which parish do you belong to?" I had more information, but now what? I enlisted the help of my parish priest.

Missing Puzzle Pieces

COMMONWEALTH OF PENNSYLVANIA

DEPARTMENT OF HEALTH
VITAL STATISTICS

DATE OF BIRTH	10-30-48	FILE NO.	191648-48
PLACE OF BIRTH	PITTSBURGH	DATE FILED	11-4-48
COUNTY OF BIRTH	ALLEGHENY	DATE ISSUED	3-13-80

SUBJECT	CLARA MARIE BETTS	SEX	FEMALE
FATHER BIRTHPLACE	JAMES MCGOEY NEW ROCHELLE, NY	AGE	34
MOTHER BIRTHPLACE	SHIRLEY MAE BETTS ERIE, PA	AGE	22

NOTICE
This is not a copy of the birth record as it is presently filed. This a copy of the record prior to amendment of _____1-24-50_____

DATE ISSUED

This is to certify that this is a true copy of the record which is on file in the Pennsylvania Department of Health, in accordance with Act 66, P.L. 304, approved by the General Assembly, June 29, 1953.

Charles Hardester
CHARLES HARDESTER
STATE REGISTRAR

SECRETARY OF HEALTH

WARNING: It is illegal to duplicate this copy by photostat or photograph.

The parish name I gave him enabled my priest to contact my birth father's church and priest. With some reassurance that the call was not a scam, a conversation ensued. My birth father and his family had been long-time members of the church. They had three children, two sons and a daughter, Ann, who lived in Cincinnati. The Erie priest ended the conversation. I'll never know if the conversation was relayed to my birth father.

For the next several years any thoughts of searching were put on the back burner. Divorce, a move, and new school for the kids took precedence over a search.

I think sometimes I stumbled through some events in my life because of the baggage I was dragging with me.

Life's changes

After some bad choices, I met and married Jim Mann. We've been married 30 years December 2016. He has gone through the most significant part of the search with me.

My mom died in March 2008 at 90 years old. I was raised by the best. I never did approach the topic of my search with my mom, since she didn't think it was necessary. She always told me I had a family that loved me and that I didn't know what I might find. Now the most amazing woman in my life was gone. My sisters and I vowed to carry her legacy of love on throughout our lives.

With my mom's passing I felt I was released to resume an active search.

■ The four Zell girls with our Mom, who had just turned 90. Little did we know that in 6 months she'd be gone.
(L to R - Me, Margaret, Mom, Mary and Liz)

■ My children, Kris McQuiston Doran and Bill McQuiston with their Nana on her 90th birthday.

The Pieces Are Coming Together

In the winter of 2008, I was working at a Mental Health Agency. I had some downtime one day during the Christmas season. I was on the internet and typed in birth father's name in Erie, PA. A real estate agency popped up. I scanned down and clicked on agents. There it was – James McGoey, the same name that was on my original birth certificate. What did I have to lose? I emailed him. I stated I was looking for a James McGoey, born in New Rochelle, NY, and some other pertinent information.

After what seemed like an eternity, I got an email back, "I might be the person you're looking for." My number is…. I responded, "If James McGoey was your father my work # is …." My phone rang, and the caller ID said Erie, PA. I was at the front receptionist desk, signing clients in, heart pounding, trying to maintain some sort of composure.

I introduced myself and explained that James McGoey is named as the father on my birth certificate. I continued, saying that I had my documents with me, and I could fax them to him. Where do we go from here?

I was burning up the cell phone on my way home from work. My husband, my children and my three sisters, all were very happy for me.

Jim McGoey and I talked regularly. My birth father had died in 1985 of a heart attack. That information had a strong impact on me. I had waited too long. Jim shared that he had two younger siblings: John, who lived in Pittsburgh at that time, and a sister, Ann, who still lived in Cincinnati. Jim was not close with his siblings.

I shared all the information I had. We talked about whether or not my birth mother was still alive. Had she been married? Divorced or single? Was that her real name on my birth certificate? We got to know one another. Jim had no idea of my existence. I was thrilled to have found him. He was another piece of the puzzle.

My position, as Case Manager at the Mental Health Agency, was contracted to Children's Services, working with parents whose children were in foster homes. The parents had lost custody due to their drug addictions, alcoholism, or domestic violence.

One of my clients had already signed away two of her children and was about to deliver her third. Her heroin addiction was too strong; she was going to lose this one also. I was at the hospital with her when she had to physically hand her baby over to Children's Services. It was one of the hardest things I've ever had to witness. I wondered how my birth mother felt when she gave me up.

During my correspondence with my brother Jim, he sent me a picture of my our father. The day the envelope arrived I opened it with great anticipation. I couldn't believe it. There it was: someone who resembled me. I couldn't stop looking at the picture. I emailed copies to my sisters. They couldn't believe the resemblance between my birth father and my son Bill.

■ My birth parents —
James R. McGoey
Clara Maire Betts

■ By making several phone calls I was able to locate the agency that housed the records from Roselia Maternity Home. This is the last piece of information I could track. The birth date is different from the original birth certificate.

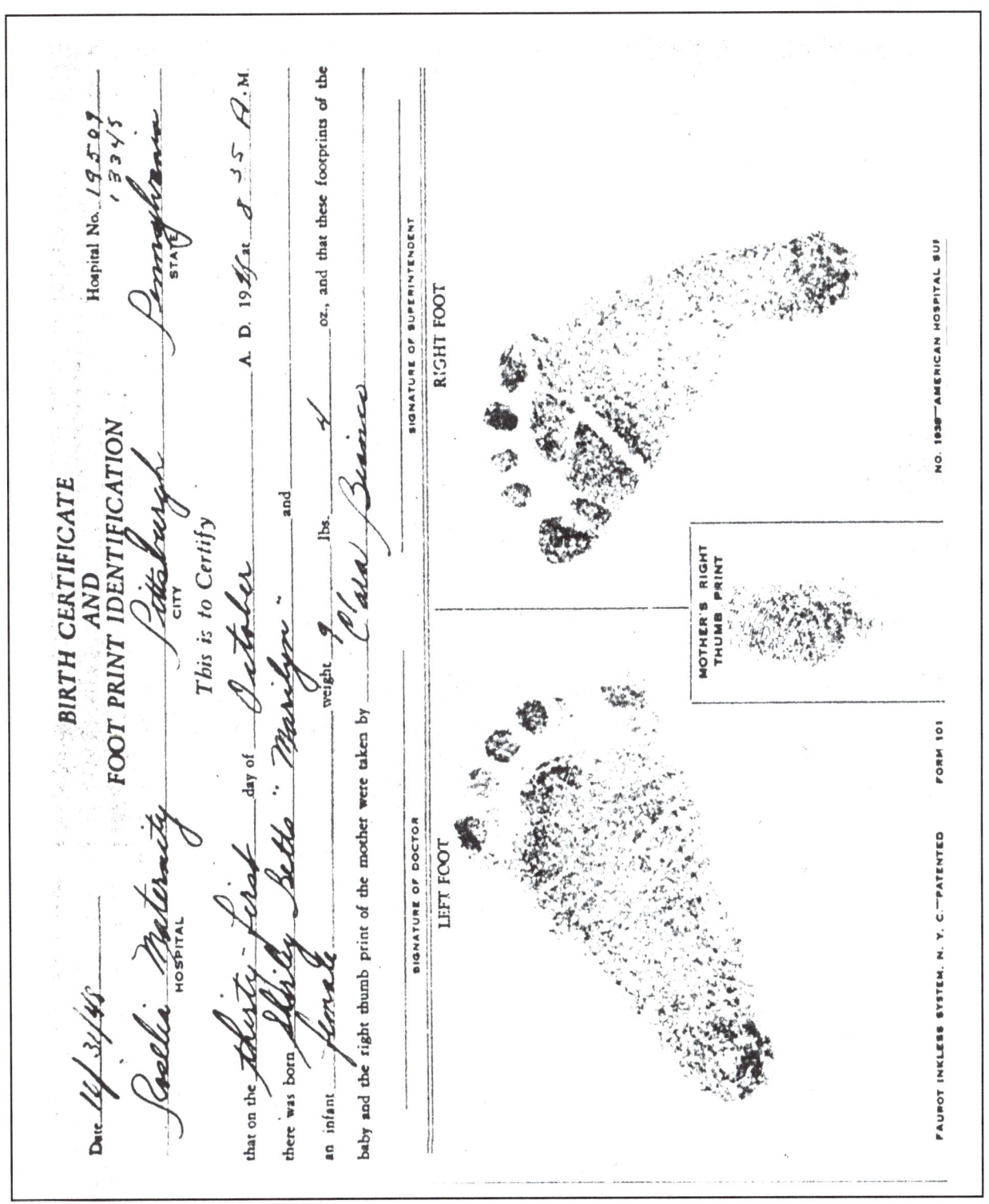

R

✞
This is to Certify

That   Ann Jeanne Zell

was born on the   30th   day of   October   19 48

and Baptized on the   3rd   day of   November   19 48

according to the rite of the Roman Catholic Church.

by Rev.   T. Becker, O. Carm.   Sponsor   Louise Demas

Of Holy Trinity Catholic Church of Pittsburgh, Pa.

Pittsburgh, Pa.,   7-31-51   *Augustine Greene O. Carm*   Pastor

UNEXPECTED SURPRISE

Titus 2:11 —

For the grace of God that brings salvation has appeared to all men..

A year later I was again at work, wrapping up things for the day. I had just recently updated my information on an adoption search website. My desk phone rang; it was a worker from the search site. She shared that she had found a possible match regarding my birth mother. The worker had made some phone calls to Erie searching a connection using the information I had submitted. The worker had spoken to a daughter of Shirley Betts, my birth mother. The worker took my number and would give it to the daughter.

A short time later, my new sister Kathy called. After the initial shock and introductions, we shared information. Kathy was a baby when her parents divorced. Shirley started working at General Electric (GE), in Erie – the same place my birth father worked. Kathy was two years old when I was born and had never been aware of me.

■ On my way to meet new birth family

■ My first trip to Erie to meet my 2 maternal sisters, Kathy and Gale, and my paternal brother Jim. I'm anxiously waiting for them to arrive at the hotel.

But there was also another child, Gale, born to Shirley four years after me. Gale had found Kathy several years before. Gale was never able to obtain her documents, but we did find out later that we have different birth fathers. Kathy shared that her mother, my birth mother, passed away in 1998, as a result of several strokes. More pieces were fitting into the puzzle.

Looking back, it's amazing how things came together. After my mom passed everything just fell into place. Sometimes, I can almost see her smiling down on me, saying, "Well, this is what you wanted."

A Trip to Erie

My children and I went to Erie in the spring of 2010. It was time to meet my paternal brother Jim and my maternal sisters, Kathy and Gale. My family has been so encouraging and supportive throughout my whole search, especially my husband, who's always been there with a shoulder to cry on or a listening ear. The closer we got to Erie the more nervous, excited, and scared I got. What if they didn't like me or were disappointed because I was not what they expected? All the old fears of not fitting in came back to haunt me.

My new-found siblings came to the hotel that evening. Several hours were spent sharing pictures and family history, and getting to know one another.

During the few days we spent in Erie more pieces fell into place. After a visit to Catholic Social Services, I learned that my adoption was private. My birth mother went to Roselia Foundling Asylum and Maternity Hospital in Pittsburgh to give birth and then to leave me there. At this point the information was limited. It was thought that I was taken back to Erie by nuns from St. Joseph's Home for Children, where I was placed in the orphanage for a brief period. There was minimal paperwork. My file contained an envelope with three

◾ Me outside the St Joseph's Home for Children.

◾ My brother Jim taking me on a tour of Erie, outside of the Children's home.

pictures of me as a baby. Apparently, my mom sent them to the orphanage in case either birth parent wanted to follow up. It will never be known if they did.

 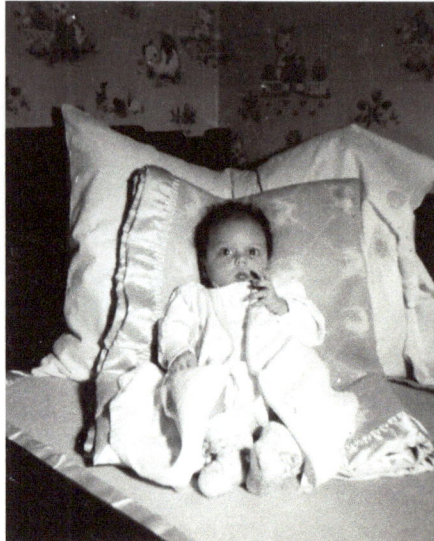 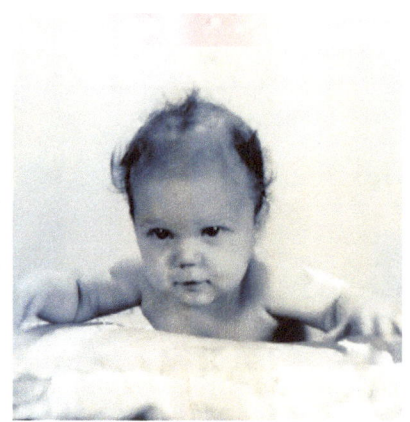

More New Pieces

The next year I met my birth mother's two younger sisters, my aunts. One aunt was 17 at the time I was born. She remembered the pregnancy, my birth, and the adoption. Their family was assured the baby was adopted by a good family.

I asked whether, if I had never found my sister Kathy, would my aunt have ever divulged the secret of my existence. Her answer was "No"; she would have taken it to the grave. Family business was rarely discussed in those days.

The Final Pieces

As I mentioned before, my brother Jim and his younger siblings were not close. But now it was time they knew about me. During the summer of 2010, I composed a letter to my remaining paternal brother and sister.

Missing Puzzle Pieces

This is a letter I have no idea how to begin.

I was born Oct. 30, 1948. I have always known I was adopted. I was raised by the best parents anyone could have wished for. They went on to have 3 biological daughters of their own, the best sisters in the world.

Even though I had an ideal childhood an adoptee always has that empty spot, not knowing where you came from. Throughout my life I have periodically searched. My intent was not to intrude on anyone's life or to hurt anyone. I just wanted to know my roots.

In the late 70's I sent for and received my un-amended birth certificate. I finally had birth parents' names: birth mother - Shirley Mae Betts, birth father - James McGoey. Even though I had names there was still the fear of rejection if I had contacted anyone. As years went by, with divorce, being a single parent, and family deaths, the search took a back seat. But there was always that ever-present void.

In the last two years the pieces of the puzzle have started to come together. After my mother (adoptive) passed I felt the final release to actively search. Since then I have found a ½ brother from my birth father, and two ½ sisters from my birth mother. I have made a trip to Erie to meet my new-found family. This weekend I made a trip to Louisville, KY, to meet sisters of my birth mother, one of whom had talked to my birth father in 1948 in regards to the unborn child (myself).

This has been an amazing journey. As I shared before I have no intention of intruding on your lives. I know it will take a while to process this information.

If in time you would like to contact me or meet me I would be very grateful. I do have my adoption papers, birth certificate and other information that I would make available to you if you would like. The aunt that I met this weekend would also make herself available to you for verification. I am hoping that you will contact me eventually. If you chose not to, I will understand.

Here is my work number, cell number and my personal e-mail is…

Thank you so much for considering this letter.

Ann J. Mann

329 West Tenth Street	90 Beaver Drive, 119D, Box 2	995 Linden Street
Erie, PA 16502	DuBois, PA 15801-2424	Sharon, PA 16146
814-456-2091	814-371-4717	724-346-4142
800-673-2535	888-793-6602	800-350-2699

Counseling And Adoption Services
DIOCESE OF ERIE
WWW.CCCAS.ORG

August 3, 2009

Ms. Ann Mann

351 Antioch Road

Eaton, Ohio 45320

Dear Ann,

    I received your letter dated 7-6-09 regarding the early days of your infancy. According to the records at this agency, after your birth in Pittsburgh, you remained there at the maternity home/infant home until 11-4-1948. On that date of 11-4-1948, you were transferred to St. Joseph's Home for Children in Erie by two employees of St. Joseph's Home. You remained at St. Joseph's Home until you were placed with your adoptive parents on 11-14-1948. The record does not indicate that you stayed at any church rectory. I do not have any old pictures of St. Joseph's Home. The building is still standing and is now private apartments. There are no pictures in the file of you prior to placement with your adoptive parents. The photos I have enclosed, I believe were sent to a nun at the home by you adoptive parents.

If I can be of any further assistance, please do not hesitate to contact me. I can also be reached via email at dstone@cccas.org.

Sincerely,

Danelle A. Stone

Danelle A. Stone, BSSW

Adoption Supervisor

• A Member Agency of the United Way of Erie County • United Way of Mercer County • Grove City United Way •
• Greenville Area United Way • United Way of DuBois • St. Marys Area United Way •
• Clearfield Area United Way • Bradford United Way • A Member of Catholic Charities USA •

ACCREDITED
Council on Accreditation
for Children and Family Services

■ St Ann's Rectory —

As I remember the story Fr. Downing, who was friends with my grandmother, was pastor of this church. It was he that notified my Grandmother of an "adorable baby" up for adoption. Story goes that when my parents came to Erie to make arrangements to adopt me this is where we stayed. One of the nuns who taught at the school behind the rectory was Sister Ann Jeanne, who I was named after.

■ My children, Kris and Bill accompanied me to Erie to meet some of the members of my family. They got to meet their cousins, Shannon, Gale's daughter and Derek, my sister Kathy's son.

■ During my trip to Erie to meet siblings.

This is my oldest paternal brother, Jim, at the grave of my birth Father.

■ Me, with my maternal sisters Kathy and Gale, and my paternal brother, Jim.

Missing Puzzle Pieces

■ Halloween party at our home in Philadelphia. I'm the tall one in the back.

■ Halloween party with my birth mother, middle back row. We look to be the same age.

I know, as long as I live, I will never forget the day I found out I have a sister. Standing in my driveway with the envelope in my hand, I knew there was something important inside. Sure enough, this would change my life forever!

As I read Ann's letter I was struck by the honesty - she was reaching out, not expecting anything in return. I could not ignore this person, several days later calling her. I have never regretted that call. Ann is a very big part of my life. I love and cherish our relationship.

My only regret is not having her in my life many years ago - we can not go back. Looking forward to many more memories with a special sister!

My sister Ann's feelings when I found her

The Amazing Transformation of My Sister Ann

At the age of 18, I found out that my sister, Ann was adopted. Growing up, I was the third of four sisters. Ann was six years older than me and always was 'proper' and followed what my parents said. Which frankly, made me look even worse because of I did not want to follow the rules and that put me on the 'outs' with her and my parents on numerous occasions. Ann would hold her pinky finger up when she drank something and wanted me to do the same .... .like that was going to happen. I was a tomboy, had a temper and between my Mom, Dad and Grandmother, I already had enough people telling me what to do and not do. I certainly did not need Ann to do the same. That didn't seem to stop her.

Don't get me wrong, I loved Ann ... l just didn't like her. She was serious and quiet and I don't remember her having a whole lot of fun. At least not around me. I was very loud and laughed even louder which only seemed to cause embarrassment to her (at least in my mind). I did do my best to try to annoy her which seemed quite easy since we were so opposite. In all fairness, I was not crazy about my other two sisters either. Margaret was also older and did not seem to have much interest in me except to torture me now and then and Liz was born when I was five and took my place as the cutest baby and I would take my shots torturing her.

In spite of all this, family time was important to our parents like time having fun on cold nights by the fireplace; holidays were special especially Christmas with an emphasis on God and then the exciting rituals of waiting for Santa. Everybody's birthday was important and spending time with relatives.

I never felt a closeness with Ann throughout childhood and into adolescence although I missed her when she moved to Ohio and married and then had her son, Bill. That is when my relationship with her changed forever. She told me she was adopted. My initial responses to her were, "Yeah, right" and "what are you crazy?" Then something hit me like a spiritual bolt from Heaven. This person in front of me would never have been my sister .... she is a gift from God and in that split second, my relationship with Ann began to transform.

Ann told me the story of how our parents adopted her and how family and friends filled the platform of the train station of my Mom's home town as the train made a 'whistle stop' and my parents showed off their new baby girl. I've told that story so many times over the years and it still makes me cry. She also shared what it was like growing up knowing she was adopted and thinking that we all knew. What a heartache she had to go through.

As the years went by Ann shared about searching for her birth parents and got so close at one point and then it didn't happen. I can never imagine what it had been like for her to not know where she came from and who were her birth parents and did she have siblings.

What I did see after she made contact with her one sibling, Jim, is that she began to change in a powerful and healing way. As she met her siblings on both sides and their families, it seemed like she 'came into her own'. It is hard to describe, I only know that she was happier and seemed more whole and complete. We grew closer as she shared her experiences of finding her birth relatives and then my sisters and I got to meet four of her siblings. Well, at first, I was happy and then I had an initial reaction to how much she was 'into' gathering these two families into her life. I told her, "They can't have you, you belong to us"! I know that we all belong to each other and daily feel deeply blessed to have Ann as my sister forever.

Ann has transformed through this discovery of her birth parents and all the relatives she has met. She is someone who you know you can be completely yourself with and share whatever is on your heart and mind. You can feel her wisdom, that quiet knowing of someone who has been through an incredible journey. It feels like she has been able to lay down the burden of 'not knowing' who she was and where she came from. She has truly found herself and that is a beautiful thing to see and to be part of.

Ann is the most amazing person. She is fun to be with and she can be so silly at times .... it' awesome! Her beauty, wisdom, gentleness, kindness and goodness come shining through her beautiful spirit. I love you big sister with all my heart.

■ My children and grandchildren got to meet their Aunt Ann, her children and grandchildren and their Uncle John, his children and grandchildren.

■ My paternal brother John, paternal sister Ann.

■ My sister Ann and her daughter Amy - paternal.

I've been asked many times why I wasn't more aggressive in my search, why I waited so long. Why didn't I make contact when I received my birth certificate? How do you intrude on someone's life, especially with my circumstances? How could I disrupt established lives? It could have torn apart families. What if they would have denied and rejected me? Do I regret it? Some of it. I missed the opportunity of meeting my birth parents to let them know how grateful I am that they gave me life. In my prayers, I thank them, hoping that they'd be proud of me.

After much thought I sent my letter, then waited. My sister Ann called in a few days. She and I met in August of 2010. We began to build a relationship. I met my brother John that fall.

My sister Ann and I have developed our relationship without memories, but starting new ones. We took a road trip to Long Island last year. I was going to meet a cousin, stay overnight, then I was driving to New Jersey. My cousin shared with me that as soon as I got out of the car she could see the strong resemblance to her uncle, James McGoey, my birth father.

Margaret, Mary and Liz have met all my birth siblings except John. My children have met their new aunts and uncles, and all their cousins on both sides. My husband, Jim, has met all my birth siblings except John.

My journey has been eventful. Looking back, I probably would have done it differently. I'm a firm believer that there is a set time for some events.

THE LAST PIECE OF THE PUZZLE

Jeremiah 29:11 —

For I know the thoughts that I think toward you, says the Lord, thoughts of peace and not of evil, to give you a future and a hope.

I've been blessed growing up in the most loving and supportive family anyone could have asked for. Do I have any bitterness for being abandoned at birth? No, but the word "abandoned" still bothers me. Am I angry that my mom and dad gave me the fairy tale version of my adoption? What are you going to tell a small child? I tell my children, if you want to know anything about me and my childhood, ask me now. I never asked, and now everyone's gone.

Back in the 40's life was so different. It wasn't acceptable to have an illegitimate child, let alone two of them, especially if you were raised in a strict Catholic family. If you weren't able to keep your child the only alternatives were an abortion or adoption. For a long time, I lived with the thought that on one hand I was that special child while on the other, I was an unwanted child.

Experience and maturity have taught me a lot. You can choose to hang onto the bitterness, making yourself and everyone around you miserable, or you can choose to be thankful for the blessings God has given you, going on to be a blessing to others. I can't say it was easy knowing I was different. At times, I live in my own shell that I created. But, it all has made me who I am.

Margaret, Mary and Elizabeth are part of life's biggest blessings. They have grown into amazing women, each with their own mission in life. Part of me is who I am because of them. I love them all so much.

I am so blessed to have my amazing children, Bill and Kristine, who in turn have given me six amazing grandchildren. My bloodline goes on. I love you all so much.

To my birth siblings, I can't put into words how finding all of you has completed my life. I look at my son and see the strong resemblance to my birth father. Thank you for accepting me into your lives. I don't see my brothers Jim and John or my sister Kathy very often as they live in Erie, PA. My sister Gail moved to North Carolina. I see my sister Ann more frequently as she lives in Cincinnati. Even though I have a different relationship with each of them, I deeply love all of them.

My husband Jim, you're my life. You have been my strength. We've cried together, but we've laughed together more. You've always told me that this was my journey, on my way to find you. We love who we are. I love you with all my heart and soul.

To all my loved ones, this is my legacy. Thank you for being a part of my journey.

Missing Puzzle Pieces

■ My sisters Mary, Liz and Margaret meeting some members of my birth family, Kathy, Jim and Gale.

■ My sister Kathy was visiting her aunts in Ky. They are half sisters of my birth mother. The aunt on the far right knew about the "baby" and that she had been adopted by a good family. My aunt confided that she would have kept the secret if I had not found my sisters.

■ My sister Ann, (center), drove to New Jersey with me to meet my other sisters.

Zell Girls Forever

This has been our motto. Since I have written this, the Zell girls have been on a different journey. Our sister Mary was diagnosed with cancer two years ago. Margaret, Liz and I were on our own journeys, processing the reality of possibly losing our sister, while supporting Mary's decision to take holistic treatments. We all have decisions and choices in our life. Not everyone is going to agree but one must remain true to one's beliefs.

My sister Mary passed in February 2016. I have never experienced the depth of love that I did in the last few months of her life. My sister Margaret was there almost daily to help in Mary's care. Liz took off Monday and Friday from her job to help. I drove to New Jersey every month just to be there. Family doesn't have to be blood; sometimes it's more. Mary did get to read a rough copy of this book. She gave it her blessing.

One of our last times together Margaret, Mary, Liz, and I shared what a wonderful sisterhood we had. We know that one day there will be one left. That one has to walk on with her head held high.

Zell Girls Forever.

Dear Ann,

You as a sister and friend mean so much to me.

I am so glad you found me. I wish it had been years earlier that we got to know each other.

I felt alone a lot of times growing up. But now I feel "family" with you (+ Liz, Margaret + Jim)

Love you so much
Kathy

Research Resources:

Thirty to forty years have passed since I started to compile my information. The internet is full of adoption search sites. Choose a reputable one.

1. Original unamended birth certificate. It varies from state to state whether records are available. Laws are changing frequently. Check the Bureau of Vital Statistics.

2. Place of Birth. Since I knew mine was a Catholic adoption and my birth mother went to Pittsburgh to have me, I researched homes for unwed mothers and came up with the most prominent one. Just in the last 1 ½ years it was verified by a source that yes, indeed, I was born in Roselia.

3. Ask, ask, ask, anyone and everyone. Little pieces here and there add up.

4. When you do locate a family member I would advise you not to contact them yourself right away. You will be too emotional.

5. Give the person time. Don't expect them to open their arms to you immediately; it will be a shock. It will take time.

6. I would suggest meeting at a neutral place.

7. If you find your relatives and they refuse contact, leave some contact information in case they just need time to process.

8. Most importantly, protect yourself. Don't set yourself up for an unsafe situation.

9. Research the library for any books on adoptions.

10. If for some reason your search doesn't work out like you hoped, "Remember You are a gift from God."

Romans 8:28 —

And we know that all things work together for good to them that love God, to them who are the called according to his purpose.

www.ingramcontent.com/pod-product-compliance
Lightning Source LLC
Chambersburg PA
CBHW060756090426
42736CB00002B/56